Filing your Own Bankruptcy

My Pro Se Bankruptcy Journey

Copyright © 2018 by Yolonna Foxxe

ISBN-13:978-1721095902
ISBN-10:172109590X

The Women's Book Shelf
16500 Joy Road-unit 66056
Detroit, MI 48228

Ordering Information:
Quantity sales. Special discounts are available on quantity purchases by corporations, associations, and others. For details, contact the publisher at the address above.
Orders by U.S. trade bookstores and wholesalers. Please contact The Women's Book Shelf LLC Tel: (734) 992-7462 or visit www.thewomensbookshelf.com

Printed in the United States of America

Cover Design by:
The Women's Bookshelf LLC
Informational E-books & Illustrations

It Happened to Me…(Intro)

The utility company sent me a shut off notice in the middle of a hot summer! My bill had risen to the tune of $3000 and some change, I really shouldn't even have to say but…I didn't have the money! I immediately tried to find services to help me pay the bill or at least put me on a plan, every place that I had called were out of funds. Who was I to think that other people in my city wasn't going through a rough time too? They just beat me to the punch.

I was unemployed and on welfare and was surviving completely on my hustle. But hustles where I live were totally saturated and the clientele was pretty thinned out. The only money I could come up with was for repairs for my car and traveling fuel to leave the state and start over…that was my plan.

I was seven months pregnant, with a ten-year-old daughter that was clueless as to how her mom was going to have to alter their lives just to survive. I did not want my kid in the dark she would have so many questions that I wasn't ready to answer. I would have rather started over then to have to face those questions.

Unfortunately, I wasn't born in a family where you could ask for help. The first thing that would be said is that they didn't have it.

Second thing would be...don't you have a man? Why on Earth is your man not helping you? The third would be the rumors of being broke about to be in the dark with your kid and you have an able-bodied man at home...why is her lights about to be shut off?

Shit, I have those same questions that rolled around in my mind on a daily basis, but the fact still remained that I needed help. Never mind that I was pregnant and have a kid. Never mind that months before my pregnancy so many family and friends were at my doorstep asking for help for their own situations, but I never brought that up and still will keep it to myself.

I decided at that point I won't be bitter, and I won't get mad at God because it's no one's fault but my own and I had to fix the problem. What could I do to make things work? How can I avoid this shut off without needing to ask people for the non-help that I was going to get? I already knew that living with his mother was out of the fucking question, I'd rather lose a limb than to do that...real talk! So, I had to come up with something effective and fast.

Not even two days had gone by and I received another notice with a big red patch across the mailing, and in big bold letters and an exclamation point it read...Shut Off Notice! Due Immediately. I called the utility company and they told me basically there was no chance in hell that they were going to negotiate with me a plan, because I had exhausted all of those options. Then they started telling me about the same government services that already couldn't help me and still was out of funds.

That was it! I started packing my bags and boxes I was out of there.

I saved my money and sold a few things that by the way still didn't add up to nowhere near $3000 and was ready to move out of state. It's gotta be better somewhere else because this city with these high ass light and gas bills...sucked!

As I was going through my things I noticed an old legal letter, a receipt that had my husband's and my name on it...it was an old bankruptcy that we had completed jointly years ago. That's when the light bulb went off.

Ding, ding, ding! Duh...file for bankruptcy and put your utility bill in the petition to stop them from shutting off my lights. With the quickness I ran to my computer and started my research. My first google question was -Can I file bankruptcy without a lawyer? - The answer for the state of Michigan was and still is...Yes! Thank you, God! Now the second question was...How?

Within in hours I had my answer and my choice was made there was no other way to rectify this nightmare without getting help from a single soul, but to file for bankruptcy. So, without hesitation I gathered myself together along with my car keys and was headed to the bankruptcy court downtown my city.

I made my way with just enough gas in my tank and money to pay for parking. Walked the long walk to the state building downtown; went through a security check, made my way to the 17th floor (scared of the elevator but got in anyway) and with my valid ID asked for a free application from the clerk.

I was so nervous I thought that maybe the ability to do your own bankruptcy wasn't valid anymore and that she was going to be like...you need a lawyer. But to my surprise she politely handed it to me and wished me Good Luck

Good Luck? Hmmm.... okay whatever. I proudly took the application home and began going through the paperwork. Oh My God! This shit is over fucking whelming...the packet had to be about 100 plus pages, the lingo was so confusing it had so much legal talk...and I wasn't legal talk savvy so to speak. But looking at my big girl, knowing that she was clueless to the fact that lights was a privilege and not automatic and with the utility bill staring me in the face on my desk, I decided to dive in and began to disassemble and dissect the entire packet.

I wanted to give in and just run like I started to. So, I just made the decision like…Fuck it! Either its going to work or it's going to fail either way I am going to try! I gathered every damn bill that I had on paper and wrote down the ones that I could think of, put my kid to sleep, organized my desk, fired up the computer and began my Pro Se' bankruptcy journey.

Man, you wouldn't believe how fast of a learner I am. (pats myself on the back) #humblepie. I studied all day and took my chances by filling in all the questions of the petition based on my situation at the time. I finished overnight; the next day I took the entire packet back to the bankruptcy office and prayed to God for the best result. I asked the clerk if I should call my creditors and let them know that I am filing. She said I could but once she sent the information out I wouldn't have to.

Still nervous about being shut off, I packed up my whole house and left the boxes for us to come back and get after I find a place out of state. I left the state and went on this long ass painful journey 600 miles away from home. (Thank God I didn't have to drive) Once we arrived I tried to find a place that was decent for my little family. Remember I was still pregnant, it was hot, I was irritated and the help in the new state was no better than where I came from. They gave me such a hard time and since my patience was way too short for bullshit...I decided within only a weeks' time that I was going to have to just face a dark house back in my own state.

My driver angrily drove us back home and it was a good thing I hadn't told my landlord that I was moving, because we needed to be able to stay somewhere when we got back. After a painstaking aggravating, hot ass 12 hours we pulled up to the house and gratefully we only had to unload our clothes and the kid and go inside and rest.

My mailbox surprisingly wasn't super full like it usually would be. There were two pieces of mail I will never forget...some sales promo for new credit for a car and a letter from the utility company.

Oh shit, now what? I mean the lights were still on, and obviously I already knew they were coming to disconnect us...why are they sending me mail so soon again?

Oh hell, what's the difference...I opened the mail and begin to read and noticed that the red strip wasn't there and no big Shut off notice letters were present and then I took a closer look at the balance it was $0.00 Zero dollars! What!? I was a little confused, but it was beginning to make sense. The utility company even gave me a new account number, because of course the old account was nil and void!

What was going on? Apparently, the utility company had to stop billing me until my court date at the bankruptcy office, and I guess since it would cost them more to go to court (because thousands of people probably were filing at the same time) they just surrendered their rights and started me a new zeroed out account! Oh, happy day! God is Amazing! Wont he do it? The lights were still on and I could face another day as a responsible mom.

This was never going to happen again...I made that promise to myself, and to God that I continue to keep to this day. Unless it's an act of nature that zips out the lights our lights will always be on no matter what!

The rest of my creditors began to fade; the letters stop coming and the phone calls too. I made it my business to appear for court and I did...big belly and big packet of paperwork in hand. I waded through a sea of lawyers with suits and briefcases waiting to help their clients that they probably charged thousands of dollars for knowledge and representation. (You can represent yourself) I wasn't mad...but I was pretty much informed...and still learning.

And because my case was a simple case and none of my creditors showed up...it took all of five minutes and my trustee asking why I filed and if I had submitted my tax information? And then it was over. I won my case...now if was by default, because I did it correctly or because I was pregnant and looking pitiful... I didn't know or care, bottom line was...I won!

My goodness! It took me longer to fill out the petition, it took me longer to find a parking spot and it took me longer to find the room that my meeting was to take place in. I collected my papers up quickly and almost ran out of the court room relieved and proud!

That day inspired me! I figured out something about myself that I had never known. That if I am determined to make something happen all I had to do was keep moving and not run away! Once I got home I sat right back down to my computer and began to research again. Looking up similar cases, looking for deeper situations and outcomes so that I maybe could help other people, that are just like me that just needed a couple of good pushes in the right direction. People like me that couldn't afford an attorney but really needed to do a bankruptcy.

After that one experience I went on to help hundreds of people with filling out their own Pro Se' documents for phenomenally small fees as compared to the Lawyers that charged thousands up front or had you paying a monthly payment to satisfy your balance before they would even submit your case to the court.

My methods helped people to get their bankruptcy petitions in the hands of the clerks within days and discharged within 90 days without making payments. The 90 days went so fast it was almost like magic and before you knew it the paperwork was done, the specifics are completed, and you were sitting in front of your trustee getting your story heard and approved.

With the right information and guide you can get those garnishments stopped and that credit card debt under control or deleted. Of course, a credit repair company is going to tell you to not do a bankruptcy that it will hurt your credit. Think about it your credit is already hurting...and to suffer through a garnishment while they clean out your paycheck is crazy to wait just so you can do credit repair that may not work for 3-6 months or maybe a year down the road.

I know that credit repair is an option for some of us, but emergency situations deserve a more in-depth swift solution. Do a credit repair if you have the time to wait for your credit to clear up...but if you are about to lose your home, lights, or even wages you may want to consider bankruptcy. No matter how much Credit repair agencies or agents holler negative things about bankruptcy...it ain't going nowhere so don't be ashamed to make your choice.

Disclaimer: I am not a lawyer and I do not give out legal advice for bankruptcy or any other legal issues that may arise in this book, on any video, through mailers, email, conversations or the like. I am merely stating facts that are publicly available on and offline. I am sharing my experiences of how I completed my very own Bankruptcy Petition in the city and state that I reside. Everyone situation and experience are never the same and results may vary. So please whoever is reading this material...do research based on your own need and situation. Thanks for reading...be blessed and Good Luck!

Best wishes,

Yolonna Foxxe

Financial Consultant/Bankruptcy Coach

Table of Contents

Hello, and welcome!

I want to be able to tell you everything you need to know about filing bankruptcy but to keep me from experiencing any legal ramifications I will only tell you what I did to file and the outcome of my experience...I hope that it helps and if you need a detailed explanation you can always head over to my Facebook page FB/fdscfinancialfitness for more tidbits of exciting information on how to Pro Se' your bankruptcy! Let's get started.

If you read my long story on my bankruptcy experience, then you already know that I had so many tough decisions to make before filing. I never even considered the consequences of filing as far as my credit report, because I was in dire straits; I needed a solution right away. Neither my husband or I were working at the time and our income was so small...getting checks from unemployment which was very minimal and food stamps from the state we could barely pay any bills at all.

I am not from a rich family nor a family of sharers, so I had to make do with what I had, which like I said was really nothing. My harsh realties of life had absolutely nothing to do with the fact that I had to keep my lights on. In the city and state where I live the light and the gas companies are merged which meant that you paid one bill for the lights and the gas. This was a headache because in the winter when you utilized your heat they would raise the gas prices and, in the summer, when you needed your air conditioning they would raise the price of the lights. How fun...right?

Okay let's get right to it. Like I said I am not a lawyer and I do not give advice, but I can tell you my experiences of how I prepared my own bankruptcy petition and how it got discharged in as little as 90 days and I only paid a total amount of $10.00 to do it and without the help of a lawyer. Let's go!

What is Bankruptcy?

As defined by Wikipedia in an online search,

Bankruptcy is a legal status of a person or **other entity** that cannot repay debts to **creditors**. In most jurisdictions, bankruptcy is imposed by a **court order**, often initiated by the **debtor**

What's the difference between a Chapter 7 and 13?

Deciding on whether file chapter 7 or chapter 13 depends on your income, assets, debts, and your financial goals.

Chapter 7

Chapter 7 is a liquidation bankruptcy designed to wipe out your general unsecured debts such as credit cards and medical bills. To qualify for Chapter 7 bankruptcy, you must have little or no disposable income. If you make too much money, you may be required to file a Chapter 13 bankruptcy.

Chapter 13

Chapter 13 is a reorganization bankruptcy designed for debtors with regular income who can pay back at least a portion of their debts through a repayment plan.

Can I file a Chapter 11?

Chapter 11 bankruptcy is for businesses only and you must retain a lawyer for this bankruptcy according to the bankruptcy laws. *See your state bankruptcy website for further information.*

Remember that bankruptcy is not to be taken lightly it is a legal procedure that can result in consequences which may lead to fines, penalties and maybe even imprisonment. Please do not utilize filing bankruptcy as a method of bill payment or fraud.

Also remember that a bankruptcy can remain on your credit file for up to 7 to 10 years, so be very sure that this is something that you want to do.

Never forget that you can always find a wealth of information online about how to file and file correctly without the courts assuming that you have intentions of abuse.
Filing your own bankruptcy is doable...You can do it!

How did I finally come to make my decision?

You could go over and over in your mind as to why you should file a bankruptcy but all the while your creditors will continue to bill you. Although it seemed as though I filed bankruptcy off the cuff, I still had a method to my madness...here are a few things that I did to make my decision final.

- **Make a list:**
    - ○ Making a list is very important! When you have so many things on your mind you may forget your ideas, your moods, your do's and don'ts and ups and downs. Maybe if you can put it on paper and look it over from time to time you may be able to make some sense of the nonsense that is happening in your life.

- **Weigh your odds**
  - What are the odds and how are they weighed against you? Will your creditors keep harassing you after they get the automatic stay? No, they receive a court order which they must obey, and they have to stop billing you, garnishing your wages, calling you etc. at least until after your day in court and the trustee makes a decision for your case.

  - Will any of my creditors show up? Maybe...but in most cases your creditors will not show up because they have more than one somebody's like you that are filing a bankruptcy petition against them and it will cost them too much money to make the effort to fight the case especially if they lose.

- **What's important**
  - Always keep in mind that you and your family are the most important part of your decision making. Your kids are your life and your goals to keep them financially set and worry free is what drive you to seek out and research ways to make that happen.

- **Who are you trying to impress?**
    - Know that this is not a competition. You are not trying to keep up with the joneses on your block, in your family or at your job! You are an amazing person always have been since birth, so you don't have to worry about people saying bad things about you filing bankruptcy...don't let it bother you. Remember what people think about you is not your business, keep on moving!

- **How will it help you?**
    - Bankruptcy can help you in so many ways. Depending on the chapter that you file 7 or 13 it will help you remove debt or make payments that credit companies may not have necessarily accepted, but through the court system they will have no other choice.

- **How will it hurt you?**
    - I can't really think of too many ways that a bankruptcy can hurt you except for it you pay ridiculously high amounts to someone to file for you.
    - Maybe if you are about to receive a settlement of some kind the trustee will take that and pay your

creditors with it...if you file and you know you're about to receive money from a law suit.

- o If you file your taxes and are expecting a refund...
- o If you owe someone money
- o If you complete the petition wrong, leave out information, or intentionally leave out information this could hurt you in the long run. Be sure to read your bankruptcy in your state's specific disclosures, agreements and rules that you need to follow so that you can properly file your petition without frivolous intent or from a lack of knowledge...either way if they catch this flaw there may be consequences. (I wouldn't know so far this has never happened to any of my clients.)

- **What financial dilemmas am I facing right now?**
  - o You can maybe base your decision to file bankruptcy or your need or urgency. Maybe you aren't facing a wage garnishment. You might not be in threat of losing property or utility services. What if you just wanted a fresh start because your bills are a little bit overwhelming, or you may have recently lost your only source of income.

- Should you consider alternatives other than bankruptcy? Absolutely! Bankruptcy in my opinion should be utilized as a last resort or for an emergency. This after all is a major decision; it should be heavily measured and discussed with your spouse or significant other if they are involved also.

- **Is credit repair a better option?**
  - Depending upon your specific situation you and you alone can make that determination. As I stated before if you are facing a wage garnishment where it has been ordered that the company that is ciphering money from your account can take more than 50% of your hard-earned pay then no credit repair is not a better option in my opinion. Bankruptcy can immediately within as little as two days, stop wage garnishment.
  - But if you are just trying to repair your credit score because you want to neaten up your credit report, well yes credit repair is the better option.

- **Do I really need a lawyer?**
    - Let me just say that I didn't need a lawyer in my case. It could have been because I was very low income and I had almost no assets to declare. I definitely didn't own real estate and I didn't even have a car payment...I owned my vehicle at the time.
    - If you feel as though filing your own bankruptcy is too complicated for you to master, then by all means get yourself legal representation. You may not have the time to learn how to do it yourself, or you just may not have the patience...if this is the case a lawyer is a very wise choice.
    - There are other options if a lawyer is too expensive for your pockets and you still need to file. In some states Bankruptcy Petition writers are available to help complete a bankruptcy petition but they are not allowed to give legal advice...only an attorney can do that.

These are just a few of the Q&A that I can think of that may help you to make up your mind to see if bankruptcy is right for you. Maybe you have other questions that you don't see, feel free to visit us in our online social media pages...you can join us on Facebook, Instagram, and Youtube for the latest topics on filing your own bankruptcy. Share us your experiences also we will be glad to hear from you.

Research

Although I have outlined my experience of how I filed my own bankruptcy in this book, you should always do your research and base it off of your own situation. As I said before my case was a simple case; I am not a lawyer, but I can comprehend the method.

It took me some time to figure out what goes where, and I had to do it all in a day and overnight. I know that sounds a little far fetched but it's true. I was determined to make a solution for my family because I was on a mission to keep us from being in the dark.

Now lucky for you...you can read this book and kind of utilize the map that I created to guide you to a simpler way of getting it done. I didn't stop my research that day or the next day...I have been studying bankruptcy laws since 2013. Five years may not seem like a long time but through those years I have managed to help a lot of people start their lives over.

A lot of people don't know or maybe don't believe this but starting over with your credit can get you employed. Yes, I have seen it...a client of mine was able to land a decent job earning good money after filing a bankruptcy. Before she couldn't get hired anywhere but mere temp services that paid little to nothing and sometimes didn't have work for her some days she go in.

If I had never done any research that day I would have never gotten pass inserting my name on every single page of that bankruptcy petition. (hint) I had even learned that if I didn't use capitals in my name on my license or birth certificate that I couldn't use capital letters on my petition. I had to watch that because I have a habit of switching up the way that I write my name. I really don't know why...lol

Ways to research:

- ○ **Ask Questions**
    - ▪ No question is a stupid question. Some lawyers if they are having a good day just may answer some simple questions. Never hurts to call...it's either a yes or a no, that simple.
- ○ **Check legal sites online**
    - ▪ Nolo.com is a very amazing online resource when it comes to finding information about filing bankruptcy, whatever chapter it may be.

- Legal Zoom is another informative website that you can abstract pertinent information from for free.
- The Bankruptcy Court's website in your city or township and district. This website is a plethora of information about how to proceed in a Pro se' bankruptcy filing. But because it is such a big site and a lot of the words are mostly legal jargon some folks tend to get lost. If this is the case the first two choices are 100% better because the sites explain every schedule, every secured or un-secured debt in detail in words that you can understand.
  - **Utilize Google**
    - Google is your friend! Bing and Yahoo aint got nothing on Google. When it comes to asking Google questions of any kind, she knows exactly what you need. The other search engines don't know jack! (Not even getting a dollar from Google but it's the truth)

- **Ask to see some else's completed bankruptcy petition**
    - If you know someone who has recently filed a bankruptcy ask them questions, like how was there experience? Ask them was it worth going through?
    - Ask if (and try not to be rude) you can see parts of their petition. Explain that they do not have to show you the income or social security number part. You just want to see how some of the schedules are structured and how some of the questions were answered so that you can compare notes, because you are thinking about filing. You don't have to tell them that you may do it yourself. (Some people can be judgmental)
- **Pro Se' Clerk**
    - In some states there may be a what's called a Pro Se' Clerk that assist do it yourself filers without giving legal advice. In my case my pro se clerk did me a justice. She looked over the entire packet and made sure that I had added the codes for exemption.

- She was very impressed that I had completed the entire petition on my own. It had a million and one white out marks, but it was correct and complete nonetheless

- **Read books on filing without a lawyer**
  - Go to Amazon.com and type in the search bar filing pro se bankruptcy or filing a bankruptcy without a lawyer and watch what comes up.
  - There are hundreds of publications out there that can help you properly complete your bankruptcy petition. Legal advice is great but let's face it if you can save money or maybe can't even afford to get an attorney, being able to buy a book that allows you to do it on your own is priceless.

When did I file, when did I get discharged?

I will never forget the day that I filed bankruptcy on my own. It was in the month of October which seemed to me like a quiet month. I hadn't heard too much from outside family and there wasn't much going on in the world.

I guess maybe everything was at peace because I was totally focused on what was to take place and kind of concern when it would be done and over with. (In a positive light)

I picked up my packet from the bankruptcy office like I stated earlier, that was the easy part.

I took it home studied it and did my research online as I completed each page. There is surprisingly a lot of information online that will direct you line by line if you need it. All you have to do is to apply it to your specific situation.

Next, I gathered all of my creditors albeit on paper or the ones that I could remember. Like even though I couldn't discharge my student loan debt I could still put the individual colleges in my bankruptcy. (For if you ever neglected to do the exit interview for colleges they will charge you a handsome fee for failing to do so...just a heads up.) I made sure to have all of the address and names of the places neatly typed on a separate sheet of paper (The mailing matrix) as well as within the petition on the correct schedule.

Then I made sure to complete the pre and post-bankruptcy classes that are mandatory for discharge. You can find the most trusted counseling classes within the bankruptcy website. I would always use myonlinebankruptcyclass.com they are very efficient and fast when it comes to issuing your certification, which you will need to print and submit along with your bankruptcy petition.

Next, I put everything together...the petition in it's entirety the mailing matrix and the pre and post-bankruptcy certificates in a manila envelope, I also included a copy of the title to my car and copies of two years' worth of tax returns. (Be prepared)

Once I finished my talks with the Pro Se' Clerk (very important to see this person if they exist in your bankruptcy office) and allowed them to look over my petition and tell me what was missing if anything and any codes I may need, I was ready to submit my information.

Now mind you everyone person will have a very different experience from mine. Some people have forgotten to complete the bankruptcy class, (which you may have up to 80 days before your meeting to submit it, I just wanted to have it in my packet so that there were no delays) Other people have had to add creditors that they may have forgotten, and they charge for this service, so make sure that you have all of your creditors listed so that you don't have to go back and forth.

Note: From my understanding and I don't know if this is true in all states, but you can add creditors up until and long after the meeting as long as the debt was not like 60 days before you filed. Check the laws in your city or state and district to be sure.

I then submitted my entire packet to the clerks for processing. It took them about a good thirty minutes or less to input all the information. These clerks do excellent work in my city, no problems or attitudes from them ever. Anyway, once they were done they stamped the petition and specific schedules with a case number and handed me my entire packet back.

Within days the process had immediately began. I had already started receiving offers from car dealers trying their best to get me back in debt. No thanks, I ignored this and was pleased that my mailings had thinned out due to the automatic stay. Yay! But the battle wasn't quite over yet I still had to go court.

I waited patiently for 30 quick days to attend my Meeting of Creditors. When the day came I made sure to have enough money to park in the lot close enough to walk the rest of the way. I had my packet just in case the trustee may have forgot theirs...lol or if they wanted to see anything. I really was just trying to be prepared for any situation that may have happened.

I had made it to court on time and with some minutes to spare. To my surprise getting off the elevator there was this hustle and bustle of people walking around with standing room only. Blue and Grey suits of lawyers holding stacks of folders and leaning over talking to individuals I am guessing about their case. My big belly was like a beacon, I used to steer me from room to room searching for my name on the list that were outside each door.

Don't bother asking lawyers for help... (some anyway)
"Excuse me," I asked a woman that was dressed in business attire, for sure she was someone's lawyer.
She smiled at me and said," Hello, how can I help you?"
Pleased that she was friendly I quickly asked.
"How do you know which door to go into?"

"Where's your lawyer," she politely asked

"Oh, I did my own bankruptcy," I proudly told her.

Her smile turned into a frown real fast and she pointed around the room and said, "Just look by one of these doors, there's a list, look for your name." and then walked away.

OOOhkay. I was still grateful for her help and was able to locate the room I was to have my trial. It hadn't started yet; there were more people of course sitting inside. Chairs were pressed against the walls all around the entire room with one desk that extended outward with the trustee on one side and the petitioner on the other. The Trustee was equipped with a computer a phone, an intercom system and stacks of files at their side.

I patiently watched everyone speak with the trustee once it got started. Some people had lawyers and fewer people were filing on their own. When it was my turn the trustee took one look at me...her stare was that of confusion. She paused and then tapped on the computer's keyboard for a second and then looked up at me again and asked,

"Why are you filing bankruptcy?"

"Because I am low income and cannot afford to pay my bills right now," I humbly told her

"Did you submit two years of tax returns?" she rebutted

"Yes...yes, I did,"

"Okay, you're good." She assured

"I can go?" I asked her with a feeling of relief and excitement that I was trying my best not to show.

"Yes...Next!" she demanded

Once I was done...I took my last bankruptcy class certificate right up to the 17th floor again, because everything was in the same building and I didn't want to come back for anything. I prayed the whole time in the elevator thanking God for this being over. I gave my certification to the clerk and asked her when I was going to be discharged. She tapped on her computer's keyboard and was able to tell me right then when I would be discharged.

Finally, I was able to breathe knowing that I had won my case. Knowing that we were going to have lights from now on; it made me feel good inside. Knowing that I would never go through this process again with a lot of faith and restructuring of my lifestyle and habits. It was a lengthy process but well worth the lesson and well worth the do over.

All in all, from start to finish and because I was dedicated to the process...it took me every bit of 60 days to complete my bankruptcy process.

- Picked up my free packet from the court house in October of 2013
- Successfully completed and submitted my petition in October
- Waited 30 days for my court date which was in November
- Waited another 30 days to be discharged which was the beginning of December.

Like I said I had a fire under me of urgency that kept me dedicated to the process. I didn't miss a beat and I didn't hesitate to get it done.

If you put your heart and soul into something that you really want and keep on going no matter what your obstacles may be...I promise you will get things done and have great results.

Credit after the discharge...

There are so many folk tales going around about how if you file a bankruptcy that it would be harder for you to establish credit. Wow, I cannot believe that people would even curl their lips to put that fallacy out there.

I am not a professional credit repair coach or agent, but I do know this...not being able to qualify for credit after bankruptcy is a myth! Now will you get the best interest rates? Probably not, especially if you are trying to get back into establishing credit just days or even a month or two after bankruptcy.

In my opinion if you should file for bankruptcy and you are successfully discharged...you should take a break from applying for any credit at all. And if you do apply for credit find a secured credit card where you can pay a $200 deposit. Show them how you have changed and can pay your debt in a timely manner. Pay over the amount of the minimal balance and you can watch your credit score rise every month.

Believe me when I tell you, once you file bankruptcy and they hit that button with your name attached the offers for new credit will pour in way before you go to court and way before you are discharged. These are credit companies that know they can lend you money or extend you credit based on the fact that you are starting over and in Bankruptcy! This doesn't seem like a denial to me, but if I were you I would ignore it big time. The fact remains that you are starting over and you want to make your fresh start a good one.

So, don't listen to mumbo jumbo about how bankruptcy will ruin your life. Lots of people have started over in the same exact way and they are doing just fine. Sometimes you have to do what you have to make it in this world...doesn't make you a bad person it just makes you human. You are doing fine; great rewards are waiting for you throughout your journey.

Good Luck!

Life changing habits...

Okay folks this is it...this is where you have a chance to make it all right. So, how can you revive your credit from a significant drop to the ultimate come up? And how long will it take?

I am here to tell you...I have been all over the internet in search of this very answer and know that there is no special cure or magic solution other than time!

If you are dedicated to your purpose and learn to change your credit habits and continue to practice those habits, day after day and month after month you will gain that increase in score and awesome hype of good credit reflecting in your credit reports.

Let's face it even if you decided to do credit repair (which I am not knocking) you still must wait several weeks or months for your score to transform into something amazing. Not to mention that the credit repair person or yourself (because you can do credit repair on your own too) will have to mail out letters, every 30 days or more just to get the response they are looking for.

So, what it all comes down to you must change the way that you think, what you believe, some of the negative things you may have learned while growing up. Stay up to date on ways to keep your score from falling. Pay close attention to your report for errors and hackers and be careful when applying for credit. Hard inquiries can hurt your score and remain on your report for up to two years.

Don't always believe the hype...research situations for yourself and validate that it's true. And if you need the help be sure that your professional is more than qualified to get the job done right the first time. You do not need to have someone fumbling over your information...and please do not give your social security number to just anyone. Check for reviews, check to make sure the person is verified, deal with people that have an office that has been running for more than two months!

Practice saving and spending habits to the point that you don't have to use your credit. Find a safe credit union to place your money into, banks suck and will cipher every dollar from your account if you don't pay attention. Banks are another business that will land on your credit report for insufficient funds or whatever.

You never even take out a loan and will owe the bank more money than you get the chance to deposit. (boo to banks)

Budgeting is another way to keep track of your spending and your finances. If you can put together a budget that allows for credit card payments or other types of credit than by all means work, it in. Try not to go overboard with new credit; remember isn't that what put us here in the first place?

A salesperson will try their hardest to convince you that it's okay to get this or that. But you know your income and you know if it can fit into your budget. *If it don't fit it aint legit*! Be bold and let these pushy sales people know that you are not ready for what they are selling and to beat it!

Live your life to the fullest and feel good about change because it is totally necessary. Try to keep your business to yourself if you can and the process will go even smoother. You are a winner no matter what you choose to do! Your life has changed for the better don't let anyone tell you different and don't let anyone get into your head as to why you filed in the first place...it's none of their business.

Have a happy winning rest of your life!

Where should I go from here?

For the most part if you have gotten to the point of discharge you have done good. The easy part is the feeling of relief when the trustee approves your petition and it's even sweeter when the creditors don't show up.

If you are anything like me and have a drive to succeed than you are already part way there. My advice is to sit down and go over your situation thoroughly... (I didn't get to do this, but it still worked out) ask yourself over and over is this the right decision.

Consider your bills for a moment; try to determine if they need immediate attention or if credit repair is a better solution? Maybe the bills are not as high as you think...and you just need to pay them off. Some people panic because they have a low credit score and start to believe that they have to do a bankruptcy or credit repair this may not be the case. You may simply just need to acquire debt that you can positively pay on a monthly basis to raise your score.

If bankruptcy is your choice I would gather all of my bills, pull my free credit reports, which you can do for free every year. Go to annualcreditreport.com (I am still not getting paid for the mention) This is a totally free pull and a soft one at that. Getting organized is the key to success in anything that you do.

Be mindful of your options and the reasons why you choose which way to proceed. If you are facing a garnishment or foreclosure and need immediate relief a bankruptcy may be for you.

If you feel that a lot of the paperwork is overwhelming, and you just don't have the time to get it done...please hire a lawyer or to save money hire a professional, qualified petition writer. There are several petition writers and affordable lawyers that we network with follow us on FB/fdscfinancialfitness for more information. Join our group, share and participate it's all up to you.

Your journey to change your financial situation has already gotten under way once you purchased this book. It signified that you are ready to make a difference in your financial life...whether or not it's just for you, your kids, your entire family or a business that you would like to start as a petition writer, it's your journey so live it like there's no tomorrow!

Have fun researching...I hope that this book was informational and helpful. Stay tuned there are more to come. If you want to know more about filing your own bankruptcy you know how to find us! I am so glad that you decided to take this journey with us and we hope that you share with us what you think we should include to help further.

Be Blessed.

Conclusion...

In conclusion I hope to inspire others that may not be able to afford legal council when it comes to filing for bankruptcy to do it on their own. This is also for people who cannot afford to pay a credit repair company on a monthly basis with slow or little results.

I hope to encourage others who are in dire straits to regain access to a better financial future by starting over. And I hope to send a message that it's okay to fall it's how you get back up that matters.

Be peaceful and stay informed everyone...

Yolonna Foxxe...

.

www.ingramcontent.com/pod-product-compliance
Lightning Source LLC
Chambersburg PA
CBHW072048230526
45468CB00019B/1045